D1447302

HAIRY HUNKS

Also available from ABRAMS IM▲GE

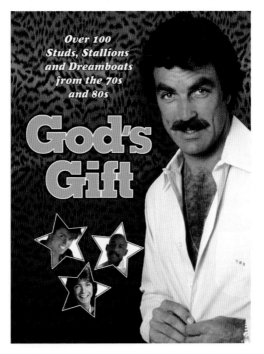

Over 100
Studs, Stallions
and Dreamboats
from the 70s
and 80s

God's
Gift

HAIRY HUNKS

A Celebration of
Shaggy Stallions

Abrams Image
NewYork

Library of Congress Cataloging-in-Publication Data
Hairy hunks : a celebration of shaggy stallions / foreword by Lucy Porter.
p. cm.
ISBN 978-0-8109-0646-4
1. Male actors—United States—Portraits. 2. Male singers—United States—Portraits. I. Porter, Lu◌
PN2285.H26 2009
791.4302'80810973—dc22
2009009330

Printed and bound in China
10 9 8 7 6 5 4 3 2 1

Abrams Image books are available at special discounts
when purchased in quantity for premiums and promotions
as well as fundraising or educational use. Special editions
can also be created to specification. For details, contact
specialmarkets@hnabooks.com, or the address below.

HNA
harry n. abrams, inc.
a subsidiary of La Martinière Groupe
115 West 18th Street
New York, NY 10011
www.hnabooks.com

Foreword

"He that hath a beard is more than a youth,
and he that hath no beard is less than a man."
—*Much Ado About Nothing* (Act II, scene i)

Hairy Hunks is a celebration of the bouffant-topped and the long-locked, the unshorn and the unshaven, the bearded and the bewhiskered. Within these pages, you can feast your eyes upon extravagant moustaches, abundant chest hair, luxuriant beards and belly buttons that look like a barber's sink drain. This is a book for men and women who like their fellas furry.

A few years ago, you might have fantasized about Tom Selleck's 'stache brushing against your neck, being tickled by Don Johnson's designer stubble, or burying your face in Sean Connery's bushy torso. These days you dream of kissing a bearded George Clooney until you're covered in stubble rash, or you get weird crushes on Hugh Jackman as Wolverine or—even more terrifyingly—the curly mop top of Steve Guttenberg.

You're gonna have to face it, you're addicted to fuzz.

But what is the point of all this man-hair? The evolutionary biologists tell us that, as a species, we lost our actual need for an all-over covering of fur at least a million years ago. The hair that we have now is largely decorative, and when it starts to appear in those hard-to-reach places, it's a sign of sexual maturity. And some of the men you'll see in this book are clearly more mature than the stinkiest Stilton.

And *that*'s the point: a hairy man is a proper grown-up. Forget all of those pretty boy heartthrobs with their puppy-dog eyes and unthreatening shaved chests; *Hairy Hunks* is a book full of real men (though we've included a few tousled teen idols for the hairspray aficionados among you). Androgynous teens may be fine when you're a teen yourself. As youths we all worship hairless, clean-shaven, smooth-limbed boy-band members. (One word:

Hanson.) As soon as you hit your twenties, thirties, and beyond, however, you can appreciate the value of a man like David Hasselhoff: a man who, when he's wearing skimpy briefs, looks as if a badger's crawled into his pants to die. That is machismo at its pungent zenith.

For example, what could possibly scream "I'm chock-full of testosterone" more loudly and effectively than Tom Jones's legendary Love Rug? Yes, the Welsh Love Machine's chest hair is so potently masculine that just brushing up against one stray hair can get a girl pregnant. That's what happened to a string of hotel chambermaids in the seventies—at least that's Tom's story and he's sticking to it. And it's well known that in the early eighties a bar of soap became so covered in Tom's chest hair that it came to life and mutated into ZZ Top.

Tom's contemporary caveman look was all the rage in the sixties and seventies, but gradually less overtly Neanderthal sex symbols found favor with the ladies. As gender roles shifted in the eighties, many women rejected the rough-cheeked, hairy-chested brute who looked as if he'd think nothing of bopping you over the head and dragging you back to his cave. In fact, these days that type of behavior is only found in the house parties of Fraternity Row. In short, in the eighties, boys discovered grooming —and then all hell broke loose.

In these pages, you'll find glorious examples of eighties "cock rockers" manfully attempting to look, well, manly, with their shaved bodies, makeup, and long, flowing, permed locks. Aerosmith, Mötley Crüe and Europe may have sung songs about doing the nasty with chicks, but by the look of them, they weren't so much gettin' it on with the ladies as gettin' their eyeliner on in the ladies' bathroom.

All in all, the eighties were a tough time for beard and moustache lovers (unless Freddie Mercury floated your boat). However, fans of *big* hair were in heaven, as evidenced by the luscious shots within these pages of grown men peeping out coquettishly through their floppy, girly bangs. George Michael at various times sported both the Princess Diana flick and *Miami Vice*–style designer stubble—not the first time that he'd relied on a beard to distract the public.

Men in the nineties took a deep breath and a step back—and the badass big hair of Bon Jovi's oeuvre became the gently unkempt, shaggy tousle of grunge. That style's natural foil was the much cleaner, but just as carefully teased, locks of teeny-bopper idols like Jason Priestley—who also sported the decade's most ubiquitous (and unfortunate) hair trend: the goatee, or "chin pubes."

This book, then, brings you the best flocculent, lanate, and piliferous men of every era—basically, hunks from every age. The one thing they have in common is that they're guys who aren't afraid to flaunt their fuzz—and that makes them sexy, and a little bit dangerous. Can you imagine Mick Jagger getting a short back and sides so that he could hold down a sensible office job? No! Can you picture Colin Farrell having a shave so that he'd look nice and neat to meet his girlfriend's parents? No! Can you conceive of the Bee Gees being bald? No! Indeed, that would be a tragedy: it's a little-known fact that they can hit the high notes only by pulling each others' nipple hair.

Let's face it, there's something a bit distasteful about men who depilate. The "back, crack, and sack" wax phenomenon made a lot of women feel uncomfortable. A *very* famous man once admitted to me that he had his testicles waxed. He then went on to say, "Well, you gotta trim the tree to make the branch look bigger." That doesn't even make sense in terms of topiary, let alone anatomy. I like my branches to be a bit hairy, . . . er, leafy . . . oh, you know what I mean.

Men should celebrate the fact that they can grow facial hair, because it can be used to cover up less desirable facial characteristics. They don't need to worry about weak chins, jowly cheeks, or acne-scarred skin. Many is the woman who's found herself pestering her boyfriend to shave off the beard she's hated ever since she's known him, only to find—once he is clean-shaven—that the beard was the sole reason she ever got together with him in the first place.

FOREWORD

Hair is lovely, tickly, and natural. Just because women have to rip all the hairs out of our bodies, there's no reason that men should sink to our level and become slaves to the depilation industry. In fact, maybe if men are allowed to keep getting hairier, women can follow suit, and pretty soon I'll be writing the introduction to *Hairy Honeys*. No? Well, a girl can dream.

—Lucy Porter

Ooh, pubes caught in your fly again, **Tom Jones**?

Black Sabbath: We never thought we'd choose **Ozzy Osbourne** from a lineup.

George Michael: careless choice of sweater.

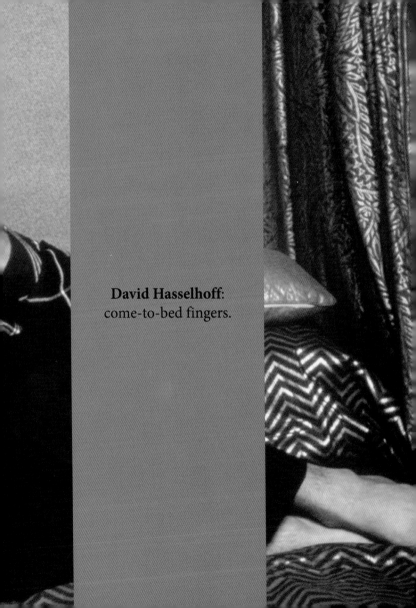

David Hasselhoff:
come-to-bed fingers.

◀ You know what they say, **Colin Farrell**: "Big eyebrows, big ..."

Or should that be, "Big bangs, big ...,"
Mark Wahlberg?

Tom Selleck, het fub

Well aloha there, **John Travolta**!

Lloyd Bridges: the amazing "wet suit, dry hair" look.

AC/DC: all kinds of wrong.

Nicolas Cage: raising hairizona.

A round of applause for **Ethan Hawke**!

Tom Cruise, that's *Far and Away*
the girliest haircut we've ever seen.

Borat decided that the mankini
looked much better without the lace-ups.

Hirsutes you, sir, **Rodrigo Santoro.**

Europe: not so much EU, as *eww*.

Clint Eastwood: flirty Harry.

43

Sean Connery: hot fuzz.

Stephen Ph-woarff . . . oh, sorry, we mean **Dorff**.

We'd get *Lost* on a desert island with you any day, **Naveen Andrews** . . .

... Or you, **Josh Holloway**. We're not fussy.

Chocolate Milk: surprising components
in a beginner's topiary kit.

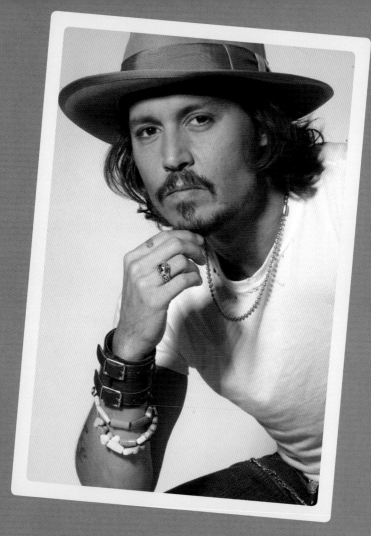

Shiver our timbers, **Johnny Depp**.

Hair's looking at you, **Alan Bates**.

Alec Baldwin: He wasn't born, he was knitted.

Just lie back, **Jack Black**, and relax.

Aerosol, sorry, Hairo**smith**—oh, you know who we mean.

Patrick Swayze: dirty glancing.

Def Leppard take full advantage of their local salon's "Buy One Bubble Perm, Get Four Free" promotion.

Gil Gerard: You could lose a finger in that chest hair.

We can't go for those hairstyles,
Hall and Oates (no can do).

Keanu take your top off please,
Mr. **Reeves**?

George Best: simply the chest.

Are you kidding, **Mick Jagger**?
You look like a Wookie! ▶

Master and command
us, **Russell Crowe**.

Will Smith: the Fresh Prince of Bel-Hair.

Sting: Please stand
so close to us.

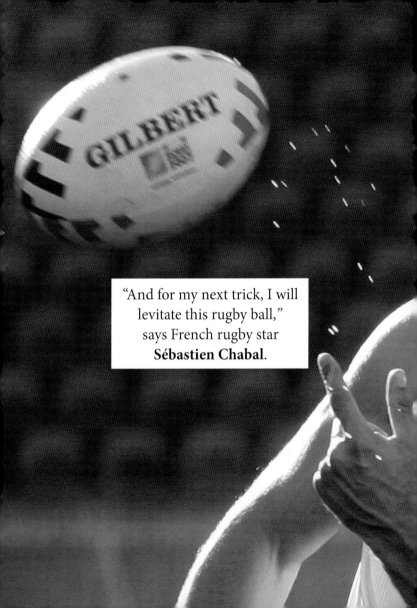

"And for my next trick, I will levitate this rugby ball," says French rugby star **Sébastien Chabal**.

Pierce Brosnan: Dye your beard another day.

Jack Nicholson: *As Good as It Gets.*

Grateful Dead: super furry manimals.

Just got out of bed again,
Russell Brand?

Steve Guttenberg: "yes, please" academy.

Antonio Banderas: a real knockout.

Antonio Banderas: a real knockout.

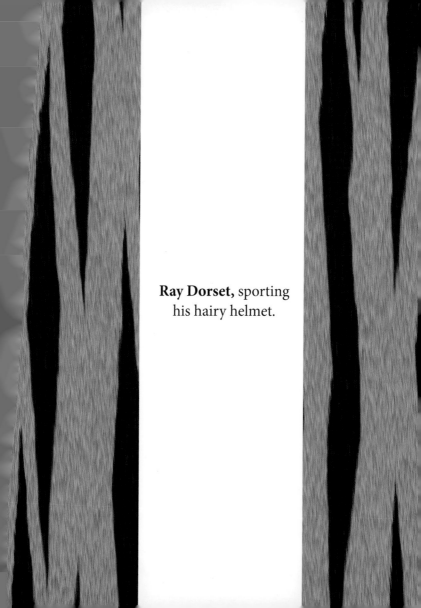

Ray Dorset, sporting his hairy helmet.

Charlie Sheen: not such a *Hot Shot* at shaving.

Mötley Crüe: nothing a short back and sides and a spell in the army wouldn't cure.

Fabio: Barbie on steroids.

Mr. T ain't going to no barber, fool.

▼ *Baywatch* star **Peter Phelps**: wavy, not drowning.

◀ **Jon Bon Jovi**: living off his hair.

Jake Gyllenhaal: worth the stubble rash.

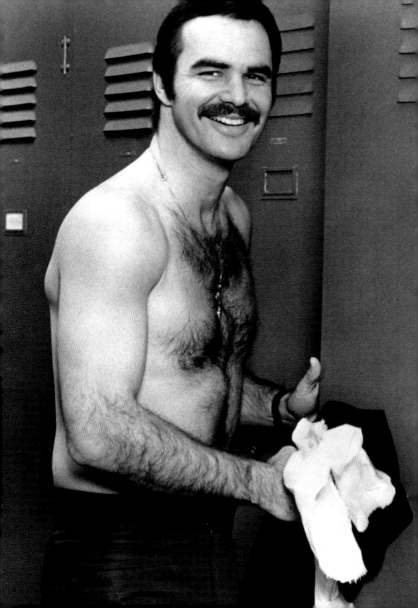

Burt Reynolds: locker-room lovely.

Orlando Blooming
marvellous

Derek Smalls from *This Is Spinal Tap*:
nice fetish vest.

Richard Burton: so good, you'd marry him twice.

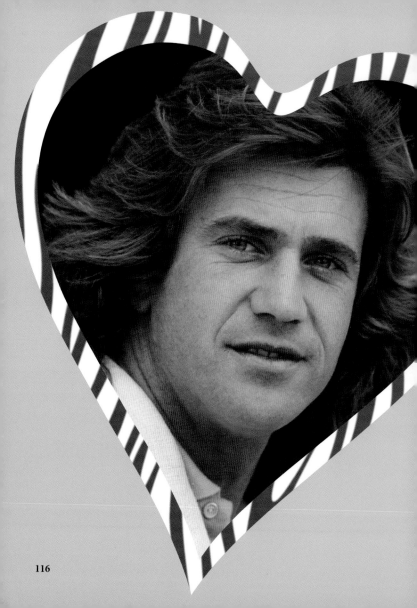

Mel Gibson: bravehair.

Jason Priestley: 9021ohhhh . . .

Pink Floyd: dark side of the comb.

Daniel Craig: double O hair-ven.

We'd like to see your Swedish
meatballs, **Björn Borg**.

Ted Nugent: Lady Godiva has really let herself go.

David Es-sexy.

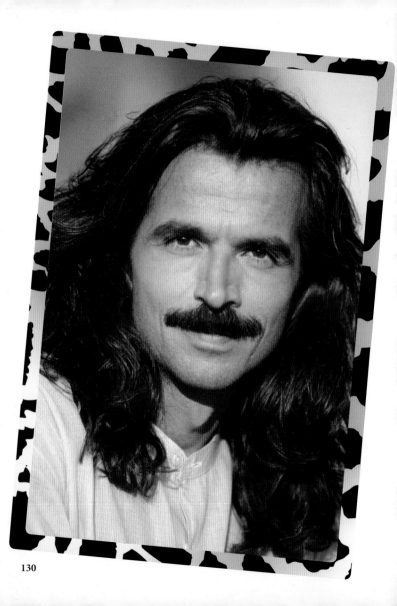

Yanni: puppy-dog eyes
and spaniel hair.

Andre Agassi says "balls" to barbers.

Bret Michaels
the mane man

135

The Bee Gees: How deep is your rug?

David Soul: 'stache-tastic! ▶

Our love for **Neil Diamond**
is forever.

Football star **Troy Polamalu**'s pants are so tight he has to carry his balls separately.

Billy Preston tried to remain calm as the electric current raced through him.

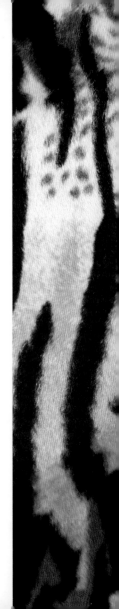

Arnold Schwarzenegger prepares for the most extreme haircut of his life.

Why, baseball player
Jim Palmer, why?

Michael Bolton: when a man
loves a woman's hair.

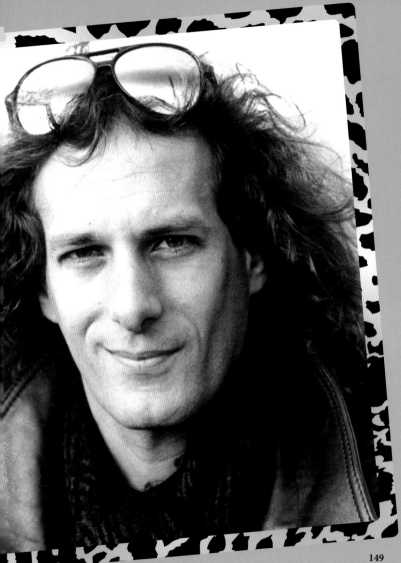

Pete Sampras throws in the towel.

The Faces: smokin'.

Hugh Jackman: Ride us, cowboy!

Even in that shirt, **Brad Pitt**, you still look gorgeous.

Picture Credits

Front cover and spine photographs: Barry King/ WireImage/Getty Images (Brad Pitt); IPC Magazines: *Chat/* Rex Features (David Hasselhoff); Everett Collection / Rex Features (Tom Selleck); Justin Thomas / EMPICS Entertainment / PA Photos (Jon Bon Jovi)

Back cover photograph: SNAP / Rex Features

Photograph of Lucy Porter: Andrew Robinson

Hunks